SYNTHESIS SERIES

Reason and revelation: John Duns Scotus on natural theology

CECIL B. CURREY

FRANCISCAN HERALD PRESS
1434 West 51st St. • Chicago, Ill. 60609

Reason and Revelation: John Duns Scotus on Natural Theology by Cecil B. Currey. Copyright © 1977 by Franciscan Herald Press, 1434 West 51st Street, Chicago, Illinois 60609. All rights reserved.

Library of Congress Cataloging in Publication Data:

Currey, Cecil B
  Reason and revelation.

  (Synthesis series)
  Includes bibliographical references.
  1. Natural theology—History of doctrines—Addresses, essays, lectures. 2. Duns, Joannes, Scotus, 1265?-1308?—Addresses, essays, lectures. I. Title.
BL182.C87   210   77-9614
ISBN 0-8199-0717-0

NIHIL OBSTAT:
  Mark Hegener O.F.M.
  Censor

IMPRIMATUR:
  Msgr. Richard A. Rosemeyer, J.D.
  Vicar General, Archdiocese of Chicago

July 8, 1977

MADE IN THE UNITED STATES OF AMERICA

CONTENTS

THE AIM OF SYNTHESIS SERIES

As the growing edge of knowledge increases its pace and widens the domain of man, new vistas strike us which are both exciting and frightening. Although the spreading light reveals more and more the marvels of our universe, still the bordering darkness of the unknown expands along with it.

Nowhere is the uncharted field of the universe of being more deeply felt today than in the area which concerns man himself. Here especially our growing knowledge deepens awareness of the vast unknown beyond our present range of vision.

We have begun to realize that the project of comprehending man is indeed gigantic. It is the conviction of all who seriously contemplate the problem that only a multi-disciplinary approach and synthesis will produce a true picture. We find emerging a cooperative effort by those engaged in any discipline which bears upon understanding man and promoting his well-being. The human sciences, the arts, philosophy, religion and all the helping arts reveal him in the several dimensions of his complex pattern of life.

SYNTHESIS SERIES is intended to introduce the reader to the experience of using the multi-disciplinary approach when attempting to understand himself and others. We believe this will lead to his perceiving and relating to the entire human family more effectively — that is, more in accord with rich depth and breadth of all those realities it contains. We hope this will help reduce the confusion caused by the over-simplified "answers" to problems of living which used to be offered by specialists in various fields.

Instead of the easy or quick answers we propose that each individual make steady serious effort to achieve a rich synthesis of concepts developed by many disciplines. This appears to be the only method that holds the promise of yielding the fundamental answer— the meaning his own existence is supposed to have — a meaning so often fretfully and falteringly sought by everyone whether he admits it or not. The promise and its realization in personal experience provide sufficient motive to undertake and sustain the search. But beyond this, one can foresee benefits which transcend individual well-being. For personal growth of many individuals brings about a **social atmosphere** which stimulates still further development toward a more meaningful life on the part of each member of the group.

5

This interaction between an individual and others is apparent when we observe the opposite process of deterioration. Just as the most disruptive factor in society is the unrest caused by failure of its members to find the meaning of life, so the reverse holds true, that society will benefit at all levels in proportion to the success people have in their quest for the meaning they believe their existence is supposed to have.

SYNTHESIS SERIES, we repeat, is intended to introduce the reader to the new multi-disciplinary method in carrying out the search for the meaning his life is to have when viewed in reference to the destiny of mankind.

INTRODUCTION

The major viewpoints toward the two roles of reason and revelation during the Middle Ages were represented in the attitudes of three men: Averroës, Tertullian, and Augustine. Averroës, known as "the Commentator" (on Aristotle) and referred to by St. Thomas as "the Corrupter," felt that absolute truth was to be found only in philosophy, and most explicitly in Aristotle. The thinking wise man could find answers to all questions in the realm of philosophy. Averroës also believed that revelation had occurred only because of the frailties and weaknesses of men.

Of the three types of people described by the Commentator, the largest class is the great mass of humanity. The bulk of such people need revelation for they are ruled by imagination and persuaded by clever speech. Such persons need lurid stories to bring them to faith, and these stories are provided by revelation.

The second class, much smaller than the first, is made up of theologians. Averroës believed these persons to be insufficiently gifted to become philosophers. Still, they were thinkers, albeit shallow, and desired to spin their webs of thought wide enough to achieve probability in various explanations of issues of the mind. They desired to study and to work out involved apologetics, but needed revelation as a starting point. Hence for them, as for the first class, revelation was valuable.

The smallest and most excellent class of people is philosophers, whom nothing could satisfy except necessary demonstration. Averroës cautioned his fellow philosophers that, even though they did not need revelation, they should not criticize its use by the first two groups. To bring undue attention to the philosophers' emancipation from the use of revelation would cause dangerous enmity to be directed toward them. Thus the Commentator felt that philosophy was of much higher nature than revelation. His view found supporters for centuries, and, of course, it parallels much of modern secular philosophy.

At the opposite extreme from Averroës was Tertullian. This father of the Church proclaimed the essentiality of revelation and the faulty wisdom of philosophy. He upheld revelation and condemned Greek learning (i.e., philosophy) in these words:

> What indeed has Athens to do with Jerusalem? What concord is there between the Academy and the Church? What between heretics and Christians? Our instruction comes from the porch of Solomon who had himself taught that the Lord should be sought in simplicity of heart. Away with all attempts to produce a mottled Christianity of Stoic, Platonic and dialectic composition! We want no curious disputation after possessing Christ Jesus, no inquisition after enjoying the Gospel! With our faith, we desire no further belief. For this is our

8

palmary faith, that there is nothing which we ought to believe besides![1]

Without equivocation, Tertullian laid down his blanket condemnation of philosophy as if no Greek philosopher had ever said anything true concerning the nature of God (or anything else!). This view, too, has a modern parallel in denominations that shun education and rely on the Bible alone as *the* guide to life.

Midway between the extremes of Averroës and Tertullian, between the exaltation of philosophy and the utter reverence for revelation, was the position maintained by Augustine, He sought a middle ground of harmony, a stance which could use the manifold gifts of reason and religion. Augustine, the bishop of Hippo, proclaimed that there could be no real contradiction between reason and revelation, for God is the author of both and he is not the author of confusion.

Augustine taught that although one cannot arrive at faith if one begins with reason, still, after the "leap of faith" has been made, reason or philosophy is competent tn explain satisfactorily the dogmas of faith. The mind can enlighten and bring into understanding what has heretofore been a matter "only" of belief. It is uncertain from his writings, however, whether Augustine felt that reason could demonstrate all the axioms of doctrine or whether he believed that some dogmas were not amenable to methodical philosophical analysis.

At any rate, later theologians — safely reckoned

as within the Augustinian camp — developed both possibilities. St. Anselm taught that philosophy is but the secular handmaiden of theology, that philosophy could be defined as the rational explanation of religion, with no other function. Its competency is sufficient to explain all dogmas. On the other hand, Gaunilon, medieval commentator on and critic of Anselm's ontological argument for the existence of God, felt that while certain things might be explained by reason, that faculty is ill fitted for demonstrations of many items of belief.

John Duns Scotus occupied a place within the broad middle way structured by Augustine, drawing upon both reason and revelation. For Scotus, philosophy was not an opponent but an aid to faith. If one were to draw a diagram to show the roles Scotus assigned to reason and revelation, one would have to draw two circles whose circumferences overlap one another by approximately a quarter of the area of each. One circle would represent reason or philosophy; the other, faith, revelation, or religion. It would, of course, be impossible to delimit exactly the area of overlap, yet it is clear from Scotus' writings that while he felt a certain portion of philosophy is autonomous, such as logic and epistemology, there is that within philosophy — metaphysics, ethics, and so forth — which investigates material that is also covered by revelation.

It was in this area of overlap, where reason and revelation meet, that John Duns Scotus, the *doctor subtilis,* developed his natural theology.

His system, a refinement and elaboration of certain generally Thomistic positions, produced perhaps the finest arguments ever set forth for the existence of God and assertions about some aspects of his nature. Scotus was one with those of his tradition who held that knowledge is ultimately an indivisible unity. He desired to give system to the confusing welter of conflicting theories that were then prevalent and to criticize the weaknesses which he felt to be inherent in the doctrines of those who professed to be followers of Thomas Aquinas. Harris has said:

> It was the task of Scotus to clear up all the confused issues and to formulate a definite and coherent criticism of the doctrine of his great rival, and at the same time to lay down an opposition, a connected system which would serve as an alternative to that of the Angelic Doctor.[2]

Perhaps. What Harris missed, however, is that Scotus was usually criticizing not Aquinas but Henry of Ghent, Godfrey of Fontaines, or Giles of Rome. Seldom did he directly confront Aquinas. Even when he seems to be attacking a "Thomist" position, it turns out that Giles, not Aquinas, is his adversary.

Nit-picking Scholastic though he was, Scotus developed the Thomistic arguments for God's existence into more cogently logical weapons than there had ever been in the hands of St. Thomas. If one wishes to read Aquinas' proofs in their most perfect form, one should read them as restated by Scotus.

Reading the texts of Scotus' work is not easy, however; he is often obscure and all but unintelligible because of his subtle discussions and distinctions. His subtleties are deep and his terminology is barbarous. His manner of writing is commonly obscure, redundant, and verbose. He forever balances upon a razor edge of distinction, poised between two conflicting opinions. Hence anyone who wishes to systematize an element of Scotus' thought must often rearrange the material, for the bricks of the Scotistic system are deeply buried under a huge overlay of verbiage.

That is the task of this essay: to sort out and track down the meaning embedded in Scotus' writings on natural theology as he moves from epistemology to God and to God's nature. It is not an easy journey. False starts and wrong paths may hinder progress, but those who follow the later course may profit even from these mistakes.

The life of this extraordinary thinker is quickly summarized. John Duns Scotus was born about 1266 and died in 1308. Although his birthplace is unknown, two rival traditions (neither of which is medieval in origin) indicate that he was of Scots origin. One source claims that Scotus entered the Dumfries Franciscan convent in 1277. After receiving his bachelor of theology, Scotus lectured for a time at Cambridge. He was at Oxford about 1300 or 1301 and in Paris from 1302 to 1303. Exiled for a few months for not holding the right views during a Church–State quarrel, he returned to Paris in 1304. The next year he became regent member of theology and served until 1307, when his order transferred him to its study house at Cologne. His brilliant mind was stilled at age forty-two when he died, in 1308.

THE EPISTEMOLOGY OF
JOHN DUNS SCOTUS

In reconstructing Scotus' system of natural theology it is necessary to begin with his views on epistemology. This subject, explicitly or implicitly, has always been one of philosophy's basic problems. Epistemology asks such questions as How do we know? How much do we know? How much can we know? How can we distinguish between appearance and reality?

The Augustinian tradition, in which Scotus belonged, tended to be Platonic in two epistemological senses. (1) Although corporeal objects form the immediate object of all perception,[3] knowledge is impossible if thinking does not rise above the level of sense experience. In the *Theatetus,* Plato had criticized basing knowledge on sense data. Augustine and his followers generally concurred, although they left room for some role for empiricism. (2) Augustinians tended to view mathematics as the paragon of knowledge, and, here again, this had grown from roots in Plato.

Although an Augustinian, these positions failed to satisfy Duns Scotus. In epistemology he tended more toward an Aristotelian view. Unfortunately, in the milieu in which Scotus lived it was not proper to reject Augustine in favor of a Greek philosopher. Unable to attack Augustine directly, Scotus directed his energy against the position of Plato. In this he had the advantage that Augustine had been so prolific a writer that a diligent searcher could always find, somewhere, a statement which could be used, while claiming to be faithful to the Augustinian tradition. If anything, Scotus was diligent. Since Augustine had allowed for some sense experience as the basis for knowledge, Scotus could go on from there — so far as to assert that mathematics was ultimately derived from empirical data.

The main question which seems to have absorbed Scotus was whether any knowledge is possible. Faced by those who were very skeptical of the validity of sensual experience, the main thrust of Scotus' work was an attempt to demonstrate indubitable empirical procedures. Scotus agreed in part with his opponents, who claimed that man's quest for certain knowledge is futile. For Scotus, as for Augustine, original sin had impaired man's reason; it had limited his knowledge. Because this was so, Scotus asserted that, for example, man can have no proper knowledge of God in this life.

For the medieval thinker, "proper" knowledge was intuitive, direct, immediate — revealing an object in all its particularity and uniqueness (*quiddity*). Proper knowledge revealed an object precisely as *this* essence in all its ramifications. Such proper knowledge would enable a thinker to deduce or infer from it everything necessary for complete understanding. It was this state which Scotus felt is impossible for man in his fallen condition. Scotus believed that, ultimately, man can have no proper concept of anything. At most, one might have some "intuitive concept of fellow creatures," but this concept would be indistinct, known only as existent here and now, and not really understood. He was thus less confident than Aquinas of the scope and powers of human reasoning.[4]

What Scotus meant by "knowing" something involved a distinction (he was forever making them) between direct, intuitive cognition (knowledge of existence) and indirect, abstractive cognition (knowledge of universals). Thus knowing for him did not mean "I see you" but "I know you in your essence." He thus delimited the scope of the concept "knowledge" because of his theological viewpoint on man's imperfection, but he allowed for "knowing" things in a confused way,

15

enabling abstractions to be formed from confused images so as to allow one to perform acts of reasoning.

This confused knowledge is conceptual, abstractive, discursive.[5] It never provides an intuitive, immediate relation to the subject. Scotus admitted that there had been examples of intuitive knowledge, however. The Apostle Paul, for instance, had known the mind of God intuitively, but his revelatory writing was received by believers discursively. This was a distinction previously made by the Jewish theologian Moses Maimonides, who had taught that Moses the Teacher received revelation intuitively, but not those whom he taught. Maimonides had pointed out the inherent difficulty, which is that believers must take on trust the statement of any individual, Paul or Moses, that he has had an intuitive experience.

But Scotus insisted that just because we can know nothing precisely, such as "this essence," does not mean that we can know nothing. Even though there are no intuitive concepts, man can abstract *some* knowledge. On this point Scotus followed Aquinas, who had accepted Aristotle, that an analysis of man's natural knowledge must recognize a distinction between sensation and intellect. They all agreed that sensation and intellect have objects proper to each. Sensation is concerned with singulars while the intellect is concerned with universals. Sensation has direct, immediate knowledge of singulars. It may be said to intuit them.

At this point, however, Scotus had to part company with the other two men. Aquinas had said that the intellect needed an intervening agent, called the "phantasma," which was formed in the sense organs and which carried the sense data to the intellect, where the latter perceived the message of the phantasma as a kind of image. Aquinas had believed that the intellect could not operate without this mysterious, phantasmic agent.

Scotus modified this. He agreed that, in many cases, this was probably what occurred in the thinking process; but he insisted that this could not be a complete explanation. About the intellect, Scotus had two theses: (1) the nature of the intellect as such, what it was *capable* of knowing, and (2) the intellect in its usual state, what it *does* in fact. Scotus agreed that Aquinas' explanation was adequate with regard to thesis 2. Concerning thesis 1, however, Scotus maintained that the intellect also has intuitive knowledge of singulars, without need for participation in the process of phantasms, with the qualification that, in this present life, the intuition of singulars is only of them as *existing,* with a *confused* knowledge of their "thisness," essence, or nature. However, in the beatification of the afterlife, when the intellect will function as it was meant to, there will be full and complete knowledge of singulars in all their particularity.

Why should he have developed this theory about the intellect, working without the aid of a phantasma directly upon the singulars' Medieval Schoolmen were caught up with the concept of the hierarchy of being. Everything which participated in being rose in an ascending order, from the inferior to the superior to the One. According to this order, intellect is superior to sensation. If this was correct, the intellect, being superior, could do of its own right anything which sensation, being inferior, could do.

Scotus' position was later criticized by William of Occam, who said that if this were truly the case, then a person who lacks sight, hearing, speech, and the ability to smell could still have knowledge of sensations. On the mere face of the matter, Occam said that experience casts extreme doubt on the validity of such a contention.[6]

But, given Scotus' arguments that man could arrive at certain kinds of discursive, abstractive knowledge through the senses *and* through the intellect, what could be known in such ways? Before he could be content as having refuted those skeptics who said that no such certainty is possible, he had to show that in discursive knowledge certain kinds of certitude could be achieved.

Scotus analyzes four kinds or types of "indubitable knowledge." Should he be able to establish that such knowledge is indubitable, it would be certain; if it is certain, then skepticism would be weakened in its critical position. These four types of indubitable knowledge, set forth by Scotus, are (1) self-evident principles, (2) experiential knowledge, (3) knowledge of one's own actions, and (4) things known at the present time through the senses.

Self-evident principles are propositions in which

a simple definition of terms is sufficient to allow one to grasp immediately the truth, for example, the statements that "a part is less than the whole," "a circle is round," and so forth.

It would appear that there is litle real difference between his categories of "experiential knowledge" and "things known through the senses." He speaks of such things as that the sun rises many times, hence it is safe to say that it will rise tomorrow, or that by an examination of fire one can conclude that "fire belongs to that class of things that burn."

There would seem to be at least this difference between these two categories. Experiential knowledge results from observation and induction. Knowledge of things that comes through the senses might be called the "representative theory of perception." That is, if the representation is always the same, one is entitled to say that the object is the same as its representation and that judgments, if disparate, may be checked by alternative senses. Thus, for example, when we see that refracted light causes a stick to appear bent as it protrudes into water, we may check this by the sense of feel and form our judgment of truth accordingly, as our sense of feel corresponds to what we already know about reality.

Scotus' category of "knowledge of our own acts" is prototypically similar to Descartes' *cogito ergo sum*, and Scotus' use of it was foreshadowed by Augustine.

Scotus has thus set forth the epistemological views that intuitive knowledge of any object's quiddity is impossible in this world, due to original sin, but that, through discursive abstraction, one can form certain judgments which are indubitable as far as the natural world is concerned. At least to his own satisfaction, Scotus concluded that certainty is possible. One conclusion which he drew from this was that everything which exists participates in "being," a notion so abstract and indeterminate that it may apply indifferently, and always in the same sense, to everything that is. Here was a concept he could build upon.

THE NATURAL THEOLOGY OF JOHN DUNS SCOTUS

Scotus was now ready to use the results of his epistemological reasoning to erect upon the foundation of "indubitable knowledge" a superstructure of natural theology which he hoped would be unshakeable. Church dogma proclaimed that man is one who acts for or toward an end. Thus man must know the means by which he must pursue end and he must be convinced that these means are sufficient.[7] As an aid to this understanding, the Subtle Doctor proposed to demonstrate certain articles of faith *ex naturalibus*. The Church held that facts which have God for their author you can also be known by natural powers are criteria of the truth by which aspects of faith that are unamenable to reason could ultimately be judged.[8] Scotus endeavored to disclose the truths of faith without unnecessary recourse to divine authority. He wished to explain certain dogmas, as far as possible, by reason alone, so long as this could be done without diminution of their substantial meaning.[9] If successful, he might help others avoid invalid claims for reason and unnecessary reliance upon dogma. The Franciscan thus endeavored to set forth a system that would be consistent with human reason and harmonious with the *sacra doctrina* of revelation.

By the light of natural reason alone, Scotus thought, demonstration could be given to such propositions as, among others, *creatio ex nihilo* (but not creation in time); general (but not special) providence; God's power (but not his omnipotence); God's truth and justice (but not a Last Judgment); the unity of the divine nature (but not the Trinity or the Incarnation); and God's supremacy.[10] These propositions, however, were the conclusions Scotus reached only after a long process of reasoning.

It is the opinion of this writer that one of the

major reasons that spurred Scotus to his task was the realization — perhaps seen through a glass, darkly — that earlier theologians had failed in their attempts at proofs for God's existence simply because the result of their efforts was not the God of the Christian scriptures. The God of Jesus and the Christ of Paul was ill fitted to apologetics derived from Greek philosophy. One can think of several reasons for this: if philosophy were sufficient, there could have been no purpose for revelation, and St. Paul tried this methodology on Mars Hill in Athens — in one of the worst and least successful sermons he ever gave. Among further deficiencies, earlier proofs for God somehow left the divine within the physical order of the universe, as a keystone is part of the arch it supports.[11] And if God could be seen only as a part of nature, the result was still the heresy of pantheism, even though only implicit.

Unsatisfied by such earlier attempts, Scotus wanted to establish the utter supremacy of the divine. He wrote: "It is a more perfect and immediate knowledge of the First Being to know it as first or necessary being than to know it as first mover."[12] Charles R. S. Harris correctly assessed the situation when he wrote that "the natural theology of Scotus represents an attempt to combine two diverse streams of thought, to fuse into one consistent doctrine the traditions of the Christian Church, with its half-Hebraic, half-Hellenistic formulae."[13]

As noted, Scotus was too wise to begin his work with an investigation into the nature of

God. Rather, he laid a proper foundation for it by his discussion of epistemology and then moved to man in his fallen state to assess what is and is not proper to him in that state. Following this, Scotus judged what usage of speech is proper to both man and God. Only after such things had been determined did Scotus feel justified in beginning an argument for God.

According to Scotus, the sin of Adam wiped from the mind of man the kind of knowledge he had had of God during his Edenic state. Scotus repeatedly writes that "in this present life we can have no proper knowledge of God."[14] Etienne Gilson concurs with this analysis, for he says that Scotus would allow many capacities for knowledge of the divine at man's creation that he does not now enjoy.

Touchant la perfection ou l'imperfection de la nature humaine . . . les termes mêmes dont use Duns Scot (*defectum naturae*), suggèrent qu'il pense ici, non à la nature prise *in statu hominis instituti,* mais à la nature humaine . . . dans l'état où elle se trouve par suite du péché originel.[15]

Gilson poses the question, "Supposons donc qu'un philosophe . . . se demande si une révélation est nécessaire a l'homme, que répondrait Scot?" He answers that Scotus would respond if "le péché originel n'aurait pas été commis, l'homme aurait pu connaître distinctement sa fin sans qu'elle lui fût surnaturellement révélée."[16] But in his fallen and sinful state, man cannot correctly know even his own proper end without aid. Scotus' assessment is described by Gilson in this way:

> Pour agir en vue d'une fin, il faut la désirer; pour la désirer; il faut la connaître; or, par ses seules ressources naturelles, l'homme ne peut avoir de sa fin acune connaissance distinct; il est donc nécessaire qu'une connaissance surnaturelle lui en soit donnée. . . . l'homme est naturellement incapable de connaître distinctement sa propre fin en dehors de la révélation chrétienne.[17]

Thus the repeated statement in the writings of Scotus that in this present life man can have no proper knowledge of God. But this does not mean that man should give up all pursuit to acquire knowledge of God.

Scotus would maintain, with Philo, that "though in fact [the divine] is hard to track and hard to apprehend, it still calls for all the inquiry possible."[18] That was Scotus' purpose: to track and to apprehend, insofar as possible, the nature of the divine.

Like many Schoolmen, Scotus was a theologian rather than a philosopher. Important facets of his philosophy were often expounded within the framework of theological problems. It is not that he confused theology and philosophy; rather, almost without exception, he used philosophical tools for a systematic defense of, or to explicate, revelational material.[19] Metaphysics was the proper tool to use in the task at hand, Scotus believed, for he understood metaphysics as the study of being *qua* being and God as the first being.[20] "In so far as [God] falls under the notion of being, He is considered by it, and that in the most lofty way possible for a science (*episteme*) which is acquired by purely natural processes."[21]

As earlier stated, one of Scotus' first principles was that "no proper notion that we can form of God is apprehended immediately by man's intellect in this life."[22] This being the case, we therefore could "have no naturally acquired science about God under some notion proper to Himself,"[23] for "God is not known naturally by anyone in the present life in a proper and particular manner; that is to say, we do not know Him in His essence itself precisely as this essence."[24] Still, the pursuit for knowledge of God was worthwhile, for Duns believed that it is "possible by natural means for man's intellect in the present life to have a simple concept in which concept God is grasped."[25]

It was at this point that Scotus' bent as a metaphysician came into play, for he understood metaphysics' subject matter to deal with aspects of reality which transcend the physical world. Thoroughly familiar with the philosopher Avicenna, Scotus agreed with him that metaphysics focused on being *qua* being.[26] Scotus reasoned that man could "grasp" God only if some concept was univocal in exactly the same sense for everything that exists. Scotus explained "univocity" thus:

Lest there be a dispute about the name "univocation," I designate that concept univocal which possesses sufficient unity in itself so that to affirm and deny it of one and the same thing would be a contradiction. It also has sufficient unity to serve as the middle term of a syllogism, so that wherever two extremes are united by a middle term that is one in this way, we may conclude to the union of the two extremes among themselves.[27]

Scotus believed that "God is conceived in some concept univocal to Himself and to a creature."[28] That univocal concept was "being," an utterly abstract and indeterminate concept, indifferently applicable to everything existent. Wolter describes "being" as "an irreducibly simple notion of widest extension that is used to designate any subject whose existence implies no contradiction."[29] "Existence," for Scotus, referred to the real world of extramental reality. Among creatures, Scotus wrote, "our only quidditative concept is that caused by, or first abstracted from, an accident, and this is none other than the concept of being."[30] Hence "nothing [that can be known in this life] can be more common than being,"[31] and so "being is the first object of the intellect."[32] But this commonness must include not only creatures but must be extended to God, for the divine "cannot be known naturally unless being is univocal to the created and uncreated."[33]

Scotus, the Franciscan theologian, thus maintained the thesis that being "has a primacy of commonness," not only in regard to the concepts of "genera, species, individuals, and all their essential parts" but also to the "Uncreated Being." [34] Scotus thought that this must be true, for

> every inquiry regarding God is based upon the supposition that the intellect has the same univocal concept which it obtained from creatures. If you maintain that this is not true [then] from the proper notion of anything found in creatures, nothing at all can be inferred about God. [35]

According to Scotus, creatures are the only objects that directly move our intellect. Unless being is univocal, there is no way of moving from the plane of creatures to that of the creator — that is, from the horizontal to the vertical. If the primary and adequate object of human intellect is not immaterial being, material being, or God, but "being" simply and without qualification, and predicable of everything that exists, then we have a way of moving from the plane of creatures to that of the creator.

Being *qua* being has properties or modes which distinguish but do not change it. Inasmuch as everything knowable participates in being to some greater or lesser extent, "being" is predicable of everything that can be said to exist and so does not exclusively belong to creatures but, in its infinite mode, to God as well.

Even though a univocal concept had been found, without further investigation mankind would still be grossly ignorant about the divine. Unexamined being reveals little, for "a man can be certain in his mind that God is a being and still be in doubt whether He is a finite or an infinite being, a created or an uncreated being,"[36] that is, whether he is absolute being (truly God), or being existing *per se* (substantial being), or existing only in another (accidental being). This is so inasmuch as being *qua* being is neither necessarily finite nor infinite; these qualities do not enter into the concept as such. Accordingly, one can think of being in either way. Customarily, we properly conceive of being as finite, for it is in this mode that we experience it. Infinite being is not a matter of immediacy to us, but, even so, we can conceive of it.

Should Scotus' investigation of being in its infinite mode prove valid, he thought that he could arrive "at many concepts proper to God in the sense that they do not apply to creatures."[37]

That finite being actually exists is a fact of experience. Does the infinite being also exist? This is not a truth of immediate evidence to us, nor is it a truth that forces itself upon us by the simple enumeration of its terms. *A priori,* we can only know the noncontradiction or non-impossibility of an infinite being.[38]

Let us start with the notion of infinity. . . . It is not without meaning that my intellect can think without any difficulty of an infinite being. Far from experiencing any difficulty, it enjoys a certain delight in this, as though it were confronted with the most perfect metaphysical agreement in which the plenitude of intelligibility corresponds with the plenitude of being.[39]

This notion is important for Scotus because of his belief that the concept of infinite being is simpler than

> "good being" or "true being" or other similar concepts, since infinite is not a quasi-attribute or property of "being" or of that of which it is predicated. Rather it signifies an intrinsic mode of that entity, so that when I say "Infinite Being," I do not have a concept composed . . . of a subject and its attribute [but] of what is essentially one [such as] "intense whiteness" [where] the intensity is an intrinsic grade of whiteness itself.[40]

For Scotus, furthermore, infinite being "virtually includes more than any other concept we can conceive. As 'being' virtually includes the 'good' and the 'true,' so 'Infinite Being' includes the 'infinite good,' the 'infinite true' and all pure perfections under the aspect of infinity."[41]

Scotus defines "infinite" as "that which exceeds the finite . . . in excess of any measure that could be assigned."[42] If "infinite being" will serve as an understandable concept of God, Scotus must now inquire whether "in the realm of beings something exists which is actually infinite?"[43] His procedure will be first to prove "the existence of such relative properties of the Infinite Being as primacy and causality [and] from these . . . show that an infinite being exists, because these relative properties pertain exclusively to a being that is infinite."[44]

The *doctor subtilis* avers that he will show that

"in the realm of beings something actually exists which is simply first by every primacy that includes no imperfection."[45] He will deal with both efficient and final causation and preeminence. Scotus goes on to lay out his course of action. "Secondly, I shall show that what is first in virtue of one kind of primacy is also first in virtue of the others. And thirdly, I shall show that this triple primacy pertains to but one nature."[46]

Among the many modalities of being *qua* being is couplet possible-necessary.[47] Scotus will demonstrate the necessity for rational thought to posit three types of necessary beings, then to prove that these necessary beings are existent, and, lastly, that they are not three but one.

Scotus first turns to the order of efficient causation. So there will be no confusion, he points out that his argument concerns not *accidentialiter ordinata* but *essentialiter ordinata*.[48] Then he sets forth the declarations to be proved.

1. Something is first.
2. It cannot be caused.
3. It actually exists.[49]

He states: "Among beings which can produce an effect one is simply first."[50] His proof is based on the complementary properties of being, "causality" and "producibility": the aptitudes of producing and being produced. His argument runs as follows. Some being is producible, whether it be a dog or a gun or a cloud or whatever. The foundation for producible being must be located either in itself, in nothing, or in another being. Such basis cannot be in the thing itself, for that would be tantamount to stating that it both exists (for it could not act without existing) and does not exist (for it could not receive existence if it were already existent) at one and the same time. This, however, would be contradictory.

Nor would it be possible for the extrinsic foundation of producibility to be in "nothing" or no-thing, for to assert this would be to attempt to solve the question by denying it. It would be equivalent to saying that the thing in question had no cause.

Hence the extrinsic foundation must be in another. "Now let this other be called A. If A is first . . . then I have what I seek." [51] But if A is not first, it is a secondary cause and instigated by another. If this other cause is B, then the reason for it will be the same as for A. The regression will continue *ad infinitum* (if not *ad nauseum*) unless there truly is a primary cause. But regression *ad infinitum* is always a weak and unsatisfying intellectual assertion. It means that one has renounced the possibility of finding a satisfying and rational answer for the starting point of any argument. Just so in this case as well. Regression *ad infinitum* would be an absurd position, for nothing could be shown to be truly producible for lack of a starting point for producibility. Hence, Scotus reasons, there must be a first primary cause.

Scotus next undertakes to establish his con-

31

tention that there must be a prime being that by its nature can only produce and not be produced (*effectivum* but not *effectibile*), by defending three theses:

1. An infinity of essentially ordered causes is impossible.
2. An infinity of accidentally ordered causes is also impossible unless a terminus is admitted in an essentially ordered series.
3. No advantage would be gained by an attempt to deny the existence of an essential (*per se*) order.[52]

Thus Scotus will maintain that some first being, effectively able to cause, actually exists.

His first argument is this. In essentially ordered causes, the second cause depends upon the first as a necessary consequence of the inherent nature of an essential cause, as distinct from an accidental or contingent cause. Yet to be prior, a thing must be nearer the beginning. This would be impossible if a series were infinite. Also, in an infinity of essential causes, cause itself would be a part of the series; that is, cause would be its own cause, a conclusion earlier shown to be untenable. Then, too, since essentially ordered causes exist simultaneously, if an infinite number of such causes concurred to produce some effect, it would follow that an infinite number would simultaneously cause this effect. Scotus remarks that "no philosopher assumes this."[53] A further argument he deduces is that to have the power to produce something does not imply imperfection, hence such ability may exist without imperfection. But if every cause depends upon some prior cause, then efficiency is never found without imperfection.

The essential series as a whole, then, is finite and issues from something which itself is uncaused, "and this I call the first efficient cause." [54] "And so A becomes evident from these . . . arguments." [55]

The second proposition is demonstrated in this way. An infinite succession of accidental causes is possible only if this chain exists in virtue of some nature of infinite duration on which the whole succession and every part within it depends. An infinite regression of sons and fathers is possible only if it is accepted that such regress does not make the series necessary. An ultimate cause is required, not only for the son here and now but for the whole series of sons. [56]

Scotus argues in the third proposition that it would not be of value for an opponent of his reasoning simply to deny the existence of an essential order. The reason is that a series of contingent beings simply does not have within itself an explanation for the existence of the series taken as a whole. Each member is contingent and explainable by another member of the series. If each individual is contingent, however, the series is contingent and, consequently, unexplainable by itself. An accidental order is unperpetuable except through that which is fixed, permanent, and itself noncontingent. "This follows," writes Scotus, "from proposition B." [57]

The Franciscan now moves to his second major argument in his attempt to prove the existence of a first efficient cause: the uncaused nature of the first cause. He has demonstrated to his own satisfaction that "among beings which can produce an effect one is simply first." [58] His next contention is that "among those things which can produce an effect, that which is simply first is itself incapable of being caused." [59]

This conclusion would seem to be obvious. If it could cause only in virtue of something else, or if it could be produced, the argument would be back at its starting position, faced by another infinite regress. One would again have to go back until he had reached some "being which cannot be produced and yet independently is able to produce an effect." [60] Yet Scotus has already reached this point, hence the first cause is uncaused. Consequently, "if such a being cannot be produced, it has no causes whatsoever." [61]

The third major conclusion of Scotus in his argument for a first efficient cause is that "such a being actually exists and some nature actually existing is capable of such causality." [62] The Subtle Doctor feels that this is the case, inasmuch as "anything to whose nature it is repugnant to receive existence from something else, exists of itself if it is able to exist at all." [63]

What Scotus is essentially saying is that an efficient cause which is first in the absolutely unqualified sense of the term can exist of itself or it would not be first. Since it can exist of itself, it must so exist or there would be no first cause.

Conversely, if it is not actually existent, it cannot exist of itself. But if it is not existing of itself, this means that a nonexistent first efficient cause (a contradiction in terms) is causing something to exist.

> If the first cause does not exist, it is causable, since it is possible. But the first cause is by its nature uncausable, therefore, it is impossible to deny its existence. Since we are compelled to admit the possibility of a first cause, we must likewise admit its existence." [64]

Scotus concludes that "insofar as such a cause is first, it exists [for] if it can exist, owing to the fact that to be is not contradictory to it . . . then it follows that it can exist of itself, and consequently that it does exist of itself." [65]

Scotus has now established conclusive evidence for the existence of a first efficient cause. He now uses the same procedure and the same considerations to affirm the existence of a supreme final cause. With reference to the primacy of finality, he sets forth these propositions:

1. Some end is simply ultimate.
2. The ultimate end cannot be caused in any way.
3. The being which can be an ultimate end actually exists. [66]

From the fact that a thing is producible and hence dependent upon a first efficient cause, it may also be deduced that it is dependent upon a final cause. Scotus has earlier said that "a final cause does not cause at all unless in a metaphorical sense it moves the efficient cause to produce the effect."[67] Thus it follows that the statement "every effect must have a cause directed to its production" is only another way of putting the proposition that "every possible thing has a final cause." Although certain things may result from chance, it would be untenable to hold that chance could be the originator of a causal order. This would close the door to investigation into the *raison d'être* of things by denying intelligibility to being. But since chance is not such an originator, it must remain true that, because something is producible, it therefore is capable of being ordered to an end. It would be no more valid to posit as an objection the possibility of an infinite number of final ends than to suggest an infinite number of essential causes. The objections for the latter hold with equal strength for the former.

A true final end must be as uncausable as the first efficient cause. Therefore the *primum finitivum,* if possible, must exist.[68] The Franciscan doctor believes that the lines of reasoning that were used to establish the first efficient cause will also establish the final end, without the need for him to draw them out again. Scotus also believes that the same method can prove that being itself requires a supreme degree of perfection and eminence.

Scotus writes that "having already established three conclusions of each of the two orders of extrinsic causality, I submit three similar conclusions concerning the order of pre-eminence."[69]

1. Some eminent nature is simply first in perfection.
2. The supreme nature cannot be caused.
3. The supreme nature actually exists.[70]

According to Scholastic thought, the final end of each thing determines the perfection of that thing. The higher the end to which a being is ordered, the more perfect is that being. In such an ascending order there must be an *ens eminentissimum*. This graded order of final causes ultimately means a like order of eminence with the chief cause at the top: a most perfect being. Thus the highest end will also be the most perfect being. As in his earlier arguments, Scotus thought an infinite regress is invalid. Since the *ens eminentissimum,* by its nature, cannot be ordered to a superior end, it can have no final end nor first efficient cause of its own, and thus must be incausable. Again, Scotus moves the argument from the possibility to the necessity of the *ens eminentissimum,* as he has earlier done for the *primum effectivum* and the *primum finitivum.*[71]

GOD AS FIRST PRINCIPLE

Although the theologian has not yet demonstrated the existence of God, his preliminary work has laid a solid foundation. He has established the possibility and the concomitant necessity of the first efficient cause, the supreme final end, and the most perfect being. The next step in his natural theology must be to set forth the interrelatedness of these three existents. He must show that what is first in one of these orders coincides with what is first in the other two. The prime cause, the ultimate end, and the perfect being must be shown to be one and the same "first." For Scotus, this will be a necessary metaphysical conclusion to which he must advance, for only when their unity of nature has been made plain, and only when they have been shown to be infinite, will he believe that he has proved God's existence through the tool of natural theology.

His argument runs like this. A being is not acting causally when it acts out of the very nature of its being, but rather is so acting because of an end. Now if this acting out of one's own nature is done prior to any other being whatsoever, the end for which it acts is also prior to any other being. It follows that, inasmuch as the *primum effectivum* cannot depend upon a *primum finitivum* separate from itself, its own final end must be itself. Thus the first efficient cause is also identical with the first final end. This being the case, it must follow that as nothing produced by the first cause would be able to equal it in perfection (for all producibles would be below and inferior to it), the first cause/final end has to be more perfect than anything else. It must be pure eminence: the *ens eminentissimum*.[72]

The Subtle Doctor next posits that the being which is first efficient cause/final end/most perfect being must itself be incausable and existent by its own nature. This is a necessary consequence of the separate arguments given earlier for each of the supreme orders. Its very nature absolutely excludes anything that would contradict its supremacy and perfection.

What would happen, Scotus asks, if two such uncaused and necessary beings should be supposed for the sake of argument? They would have to possess one thing commonly: the characteristics of necessary beings, as well as other characteristics sufficient to demonstrate their individuality. This would leave two possibilities. The individual characteristics would either demand the necessary existence of the being in which they inhere or they would not. If they did so demand, each necessary being would exist in virtue of two natures: one common, one individual. But this would be incomprehensible. It would be contrary to the fact that every being is determined by one nature alone. As Scotus says, "In such a case the being would exist necessarily in virtue of something which, if eliminated, would still leave the nature existing as necessarily as before."[73] On the other hand, if the distinctive characteristics of the beings did not demand their necessary existence, there would be the anomaly of a set of beings both partially necessary and partially unnecessary, but "any entity which is not of itself necessary being is only possible being. Nothing merely possible, however, is included in what exists necessarily."[74]

The Franciscan next affirms that if two necessary beings exist, this would mean that all else would be dependent upon two varying, ultimate, and independent ends. All sensible things would be split and torn apart by the division, "for what is ordered to one ultimate end cannot be ordered to another, as it is impossible to have two total and perfect causes of the same order causing one and the same thing."[75] Scotus then summarizes that "some one nature is the term of this triple dependence, and thus enjoys this triple primacy" — of a first efficient cause/final end/most perfect being.[76]

Scotus has not yet completed the task he set for himself. He must now demonstrate "that the first efficient cause is endowed with will and possesses such intelligence that this cause understands an infinity of distinct things and that its essence, which indeed is its intelligence, represents an infinity of things. Secondly, I go on from this to infer the infinity of this Being."[77]

It is the contention of the *doctor subtilis* that the first cause understands and wills; that is, it has intelligence and volition. Otherwise one would have to assume the possibility that the universe might ultimately be the result of chance. This was previously shown to be no explanation at all. But there is order — discernible order, Scotus declares — not chaos, in the universe and things appear to be acting for an end. Given this, it is plausible that the explanation lies in their dependence on a first cause which volitionally loves the final end. This free choice is important, for if the prime cause by necessity loved the end, it would be controlled by it. This would destroy the necessary independence of such a cause. As seen earlier, the end that is loved by the first cause is none other than itself; hence it freely of its own choice loves itself.[78]

The theologian insists that "the knowledge and volition of this First Being is the same as its essence."[79] This must be so, Scotus reasons, because it is knowledge and love of the preeminent final end that actuates the first cause to act; but the final end has been shown to be identical with the first efficient cause. And so God acts because he knows and loves himself. Since the activity in which God loves himself as a first final end is incausable, the act by which the first cause knows and loves itself must be identified with the first cause itself. Scotus phrases the matter in these words:

The will is the same as the first nature, because willing is a function only of the will; wherefore, if the volition itself is incausable, the same is true of the will to which it belongs. . . . Secondly . . . this self-knowledge is identical with that nature, for nothing is loved unless it is known [and] just as this self-love exists necessarily in virtue of itself, so also this self-knowledge.[80]

The matter is now broadened. Scotus points out that "no knowledge can be an accident of the first nature."[81]

The first nature has been shown to be first in the order of efficiency, and therefore has of itself and apart from anything else, the ability to produce whatever can be produced. . . . But without a knowledge of the latter, the first nature would be unable to produce what can be produced. Hence, the knowledge of any of these other beings is not something distinct from its own nature.[82]

By the same act through which God knows and loves himself, he knows and loves all possible beings, for nothing can be willed or produced which is not first known. Thus God must have a distinct knowledge of all possible and real beings prior to any reality they may attain, for they may not be willed without his first knowing them. Scotus states this point well:

Before anything can be willed . . . it must be known. Hence before we can even conceive of the First Being as willing or causing A, we must conceive it as knowing A, for without such knowledge the first cause would not be properly a cause. And the same holds true of everything else it could produce."[83]

Again, he says: "The same act of knowledge

can embrace several interrelated objects, and the more perfect this act is, the greater can be the number of objects. Consequently, an act that is so completely perfect that it would be impossible to have anything more perfect, will embrace all that can be known."[84] The perfect intellect of the prime being will know distinctly and actually all that can participate in the nature of being; thus "none of its knowledge will be accidental to it."[85]

The next conclusion to which the Subtle Doctor proceeds is that "the intellect of the First Being knows everything else that can be known with a knowledge that is eternal, distinct, actual, necessary, and prior by nature to the existence of these things in themselves."[86] The prime being is eternal. Its intellect, which knows all that is particable and participating in being actually and distinctly, must also therefore be eternal. Now there is but one necessary being. Since all beings that are distinct from the first cause are not necessary and inasmuch as they exist only dependently, due to the instigating action of the *primum effectivum,* the knowledge of beings is prior to their appearance. Scotus gives two reasons for this: "The necessary is always prior to the contingent, and the first cause acts only to the extent that it knows."[87]

These statements of Scotus on the intellect have been drawn out at some length for they run counter to the informed judgment of many Scotistic commentators who have asserted that the radical thrust of Scotus in this area is not the intellect but the will. Those authors have incorrectly formed their conclusions.[88]

It is only at this point that Scotus deliberately and systematically treats of God's infinity. It has previously been implicit, and occasionally explicit, in much that he has written, but now he treats it as a subject in itself. He has waited to explicate it, for he believed it necessary to investigate and establish the foregoing propositions before giving a proper treatment of infinitude. He sets forth four statements.

1. This Being is the first efficient cause of all other things.
2. This Being, as efficient cause, has a distinct knowledge of all that can be made.
3. This Being is supreme in finality.
4. This Being is supreme in eminence.[89]

It may be sufficient to say that Scotus bases his proof for the first proposition on his previous reasoning that the first being is the cause of all things. To this he adds the conclusion: and therefore infinite. "Now it is clear that, so far as the First Being exists in virtue of itself, it has [the] ability to produce endlessly."[90] Scotus asserts that whatever can produce an infinity of effects through its own power alone, without the help of another agent, must itself be infinite, since if there is no limit to effectables, there can be no limit in the power that produces them. And that which is without limit is infinite.

On behalf of proposition 2 the Franciscan argues that

the things that can be known are infinite in number. But they are all actually known by an intellect which knows all things. Therefore, that intellect is infinite which, at one and the same moment, has actual knowledge of all these things. Now such is the intellect of the First Being."[91]

Since even before it can produce, it must know, and since there is an infinity of intelligible beings to be known, it is necessary to say that any intellect that is capable of knowing perfectly the whole gamut of possibilities must itself be infinite.

Concerning the third postulate, Scotus asserts that God cannot truly be the final end unless he is infinite. Our will can desire and love an object that is greater than any finite object, and there seems to be a natural inclination to love an infinite good above all. It appears that, in the act of loving, we may have an actual experience of an infinite good. Scotus puts forth his belief that "indeed it seems that the will is not perfectly satisfied with anything else."[92] But if "infinite" and "good" were incompatible, then no way would be open for the will to achieve satisfaction. The infinitely good final end which draws us to itself must therefore exist.

Scotus' fourth postulate is similarly established. He states that it is not incompatible with finite being that a more perfect being should exist. However, it is incompatible with the most perfect being that a more perfect being should exist. This most perfect being (which is also our final end), toward which we yearn, must be supreme. Now it has already been shown that the first being is also the most perfect being; therefore the *ens eminentissimum,* which is supreme, must be infinite.[93]

At this stage of his natural theology the Subtle Doctor treats the Anselmian *a priori* argument[94]: "God is a being greater than which nothing greater can be conceived." Scotus touches up this proposition to: "God is a being that, if one can conceive of Him without contradiction, it would be impossible to think of a greater being without contradiction."[95] He states that "the phrase 'without contradiction' must be added," for "the greatest object conceivable without contradiction can actually exist in reality."[96] As he has earlier shown, what can exist of itself, as would be the case with God, necessarily exists. Anselm had been able to demonstrate only that, beginning with an *a priori* argument, it was neither impossible nor absurd that God should exist. Scotus, however, by using an *a priori* argument only after having discussed the *primum effectivum, primum finitivum,* and *ens eminentissimum,* and showing their essential unity, is able to strengthen the force of Anselm's reasoning.

Scotus now summarizes what he has thus far accomplished. He has established that some being is simply first in efficiency, finality, and eminence. This being enjoys a unity of existence. It wills and has understanding. It is infinite. This infinite character of God is, for Scotus, God's most radical predicate. More than any other, infinity characterizes God in his absolute perfection.[97] Scotus has explicated this infinitude because the prime being knows all that can be made, because it may produce all that is effectible, and because it is both last end and most excellent.

> Having proved these conclusions, one can [say that] *in the realm of beings there actually exists a being which has a triple primacy, and this being is infinite. Therefore, some infinite being actually exists.* This notion of God as an infinite being is the most perfect absolute concept we can have of him. . . . Consequently, we prove that God, conceived under the most perfect aspect possible to us, actually exists.[98]

At this point Scotus believes that natural theology has brought forth as much information on the character of God as is possible without recourse to the authority of revelation and the Church. Limited by the very nature of his object, Scotus could not claim to go further, but he has come this far.

THE CONTRIBUTION OF
JOHN DUNS SCOTUS

A great deal of Scotus' effort, as indicated earlier, was directed toward the modification or refutation of certain opinions held by Henry of Ghent, Godfrey of Fontaines, and Giles of Rome. Scotus, for this reason, built up a body of writing that often lacked organization due to his work as arbiter and polemicist. This scattering of his system and his often obscure subtleties and terminologies have caused him to be described as one who "if not the most difficult, yet without doubt [is] the most irritating of the medieval schoolmen."[99] Still, his contribution to philosophical and theological thought has been magnificent.

In spite of the polemic character of much of the Scotsman's writings, he was no skeptic. The rejection of the apologetics of other Schoolmen as deficient or inadequate was never an end in itself. Rather, it was the occasion and the means of constructing a stronger edifice of defense for the Christian faith. It seems to me that Scotus' work resulted in the most compelling argument within natural theology for God's existence that has yet been developed. At the very least, it may be said that the Scotistic argument, with cogency and credibility, takes the work of Aquinas and pushes it toward completion. Indeed, if one wishes to read the ways of Aquinas in their most perfect form, one must do so in the writings of Scotus.

In many ways the Subtle Doctor was surprisingly modern, in the fashion of post-Protestant theologians. Many of these men, such as Paul Tillich, have attempted to construct systematic theologies, delineating the boundary of an autonomous sphere for religion, that would be all-inclusively safe from skeptical encroachment. Tillich endeavored to embrace a new apprehension of God as the ground of being — a concept he believed might be both necessary and safe from attacks or criticism. Scotus, however, succeeded where Tillich did not, and the Schoolman's natural theology well depicts the being whose essence it is to exist.

In his attempt to counter the skeptical fideists of his day, Scotus postulated the belief that the concept of being, at least, is univocal and may properly be applied both to God and to creatures. Such fideists could easily become agnostics and persuade others into heresy. Scotus believed that by demonstrating the univocity of being, and aided by man's internal and external experiences, reason could go on to recognize God's existence and his necessary attributes.

The *doctor subtilis* gave service to Augustine's comment that although God is above mind, he is to be sought after. At the same time, Scotus expressed his conviction that although, strictly speaking, God is unknown precisely as this essence to man in the present life, that is not to say that he is absolutely unknowable.

Scotus felt that revelation was absolutely necessary for any adequate knowledge of God. At the same time, he held the philosophical field of metaphysics to be a great and competent aid for expounding certain Christian doctrines. Impelled to his task as a result of his desire to provide an intellectual apologetic against fideism, Scotus ended with a system which viewed philosophy as extremely limited in the number of Christian truisms it could demonstrate.

Perhaps Scotus was hardly aware of the results of his work, yet his delimitation of philosophy to a smaller realm than had been allowed by previous thinkers and his undercutting of many previously accepted theories gave impetus to those who would further limit its role. In his gibes at too-easy acceptance of weak "proofs" — when he asserted that philosophy is unable to demonstrate many attributes of God — when he denied its use in proving the immortality of the soul and other doctrines — made a road straight for the later work of Occam.

Of the philosophical systems of natural theology set up by such men as Anselm, Bonaventure, Albertus Magnus, and Aquinas, very little remained after William of Occam completed his work. Little remained save for the golden way to God laid out by John Duns Scotus.

NOTES

I am deeply indebted to those who have read and criticized this manuscript and who have helped me correct it at many points. Any excellence it has is due to their expertise and interest. Any remaining difficulties bear my own "imprimatur." I would like to pay particular tribute to Fr. Allan B. Wolter O.F.M. and to Dr. Felix Alluntis, both Professors in the School of Philosophy, The Catholic University of America. Their comments, based on years of specialization in Scotistic studies, have been invaluable. I also thank my former colleague, Fr. Robert J. Burke, and Dr. Roy Van Neste, Assistant Professor of Medieval History, of the University of South Florida, Tampa.

1. Etienne Gilson, *Reason and Revelation in the Middle Ages* (New York, 1938) pp. 9-10.

2. Charles R. S. Harris, *Duns Scotus* (2 vols.; Oxford, 1877) 1:302. Harris' work is still useful, although it must be read with caution, for it is not only old but on many points is far from reliable, for it is based in part on works since shown to be inauthentic.

3. Cf. Thomas Aquinas' theory on accidental and substantial modification.

4. On the distinction between quidditative and essential knowledge, Thomas Aquinas claimed only essential knowledge of God (potential, the result of reason, which suggests essence, as opposed to actual, the result of composition [quiddity] and division [accidens], which suggest explicit existence and implicit essence).

5. For more on "confused knowledge," see Camille Bérube, *La Connaissance de l'Individuel au Moyen Age* (Montreal: Presses de Université de Montreal et Paris, Presses Universitaires de France, 1964). Two chapters are devoted to Scotus' theory and various misinterpretations of it by historians of philosophy.

6. It is interesting to note, in this connection, recent experiments in psychology which seem to suggest that

51

color impressions may occur through use of the tactile sense alone. And a recent note in *Medical World News* (XVII, 10) reports that after medical researchers in England removed a monkey's striate cortex, rendering it blind, the animal later came to be able to move through obstacle courses and to follow moving objects with its eyes. Similar abilities have been demonstrated by humans whose visual cortexes have been damaged. A possible explanation is that optic nerves also connect to the superior colliculus of the brain and that the superior colliculus has uses heretofore unsuspected.

7. Harris, *Scotus,* 1:84.

8. Parthenius Minges, "Duns Scotus," *Catholic Encyclopedia* (15 vols.; New York, 1909), 5:198.

9. Ibid.

10. Frederick Copleston, *A History of Philosophy* (2 vols.; London, 1946–50), 2, *passim.*

11. This is also the argument of Harris (*Scotus,* 2:178–81). In contrast, it should be noted that some feel the "ways" of Thomas Aquinas in his *Summa* were never intended to be taken as complete and unanswerable demonstrations of the God of Scripture. Rather, they were given to show what pagan philosophy, unaided by divine revelation, could conclude about God. A work that expounds this position is that of Edward Sillem, *Ways of Thinking about God* (New York, 1962).

12. Copleston, *History,* 2:520.

13. Harris, *Scotus,* 2:178.

14. Allan Wolter, ed., *Duns Scotus* (New York, 1962), p. 14 and *passim.* This work will hereafter be cited as "Wolter."

15. Etienne Gilson, *Jean Duns Scot* (Paris, 1952), p. 14.

16. Ibid., p. 15.

17. Ibid., pp. 17–18.

18. Hans Lewy, Alexander Altmann and Isaak Heinemann, eds., *Three Jewish Philosophers* (Cleveland, 1961), p. 59.

19. Allan Wolter, "John Duns Scotus," in Paul Edwards (ed.), *Encyclopedia of Philosophy* (8 vols., New York, 1967), 2:427–28.

20. Copleston, *History,* 2:518.

21. Harris, *Scotus,* 1:87.

22. Wolter, p. 11.

23. Ibid.

24. Ibid., pp. 25–26.

25. Ibid., p. 17.

26. Wolter, "John Duns Scotus," p. 428.

27. Wolter, p. 20.

28. Ibid., p. 19.

29. Wolter, "John Duns Scotus," p. 428.

30. Wolter, p. 6.

31. Ibid., p. 4.

32. Ibid.

33. Ibid., p. 5.

34. Ibid., p. 4.

35. Ibid., p. 25.

36. Ibid., p. 20.

37. Ibid., p. 27.

38. Efrem Bettoni, *Duns Scotus* (Washington, 1961), pp. 32–33. Notice Scotus' references to the results of his epistemological studies of indubitable knowledge.

39. Ibid., p. 133.

40. Wolter, p. 27.

41. *Ibid.* Or, as Wolter says, there are "three attributes coextensive with being — 'one,' 'true,' and 'good' — for to be capable of existing in the extramental world, the subject must have a certain unity and be capable of being known and being desired or willed." See his "John Duns Scotus," p. 428.

42. Wolter, p. 72.

43. Ibid., p. 35.

44. Ibid., p. 37.

45. Ibid.

46. Ibid., p. 38.

47. There is probably an inexhaustible number of such attributes. Others would include, in addition to the "possible-necessary" (given above), "infinite-finite" and "cause-caused."

48. Wolter, pp. 40–41.

49. Ibid., p. 38.

50. Ibid., p. 39.

51. Ibid.

52. Ibid., p. 41.

53. Ibid., p. 42.

54. Ibid.

55. Ibid., p. 43.
56. Ibid.
57. Ibid., p. 44.
58. Ibid., p. 39.
59. Ibid., p. 45.
60. Ibid.
61. Ibid.
62. Ibid., p. 46.
63. Ibid.
64. Bettoni, *Scotus,* p. 142.
65. Wolter, p. 47.
66. Ibid., pp. 47–48.
67. Ibid., p. 45.
68. Ibid., p. 48.
69. Ibid.
70. Ibid., pp. 48–49.
71. Ibid.
72. Ibid., p. 49.
73. Ibid., p. 51.
74. Ibid.
75. Ibid.
76. Ibid., p. 52.
77. Ibid.
78. Ibid., pp. 55–56.
79. Ibid., p. 56.
80. Ibid., p. 58.
81. Ibid.
82. Ibid.
83. Ibid., p. 59.
84. Ibid.
85. Ibid.
86. Ibid., pp. 60–61.
87. Ibid.
88. A list of some who stress that the radical thrust of Scotus' argument emphasizes the will of the prime Being would include Minges, "Scotus"; Gilson, *Scot;* Harris, *Scotus;* and Dorothea Sharp, *Franciscan Philosophy at Oxford in the Thirteenth Century* (Oxford, 1930).
89. Wolter, p. 62.
90. Ibid.
91. Ibid., p. 68.
92. Wolter, p. 71.
93. Ibid.

94. Ibid., pp. 73–74.
95. Ibid., p. 73.
96. Ibid.
97. Ibid., pp. 75–76.
98. Ibid., p. 76.
99. Harris, *Scotus,* 1:266–67.

EXISTENTIALISM AND ITS IMPLICATIONS FOR COUNSELING .65

M. Emmanuel Fontes

A study in depth which leads to seven general principles for integrating existential insights into counseling.

THE CREATION OF FULL HUMAN PERSONALITY .65

Joseph Drew & William Hague

Complete psychological growth is a process inseparable from total reality—biological and spiritual, internal and external. Vocation is important.

SEX AND EXISTENCE .65

Adrian van Kaam

This booklet describes psychological, social and religious factors which hinder or promote the integration of sex and human existence.

NEW EDUCATIONAL METHODS FOR INCREASING RELIGIOUS EFFECTIVENESS .65

Dean C. Dauw

Special group methods of self-education that have proved helpful to others are also helpful to religious organizations.

LOVE AND SELFISHNESS .65

Alice von Hildebrand

True love cannot be separated from a joyful readiness to make enduring sacrifices for the sake of the beloved.

PERSONAL IDENTITY AND RELIGIOUS COMMITMENT .65

Francis Forde

Religious commitment calls for a mature judgement and consistent fidelity and creative care.

NEW LOOK CELIBACY .65

Rosemary Haughton

A vocation to celibacy is a sign of the Christian orientation toward the eternal life. This booklet reveals its larger dimension.

A PSYCHOLOGY OF THE CATHOLIC INTELLECTUAL .... .65
Adrian van Kaam

The split between secular and religious learning rooted in psychological history must be healed to prevent disaster.

EMOTIONAL DEVELOPMENT AND SPIRITUAL GROWTH .... .65
Timothy J. Gannon

To what extent can insights into a man's emotional life contribute to the solution of problems of spiritual growth.

LITURGY IN ADOLESCENT PERSONALITY GROWTH .... .65
Marygrace McCullough

The Liturgy does contain personality building forces that can be used effectively on the adolescent level.

PSYCHOLOGICAL DEVELOPMENT AND THE CONCEPT OF MORTAL SIN .... .65
Robert O'Neil & Michael Donovan

This booklet challenges the premise of current sacramental and educational practice that children can be guilty of mortal sin at the age of seven.

THE ADDICTIVE PERSONALITY .... .65
Adrian van Kaam

A psychological study of the origin, structure and function of the personality prone to addiction.

SPIRITUALITY THROUGH THE AGES .... .65

Our understanding of God and his love has shifting emphases. The contour and quality of our response will vary from time to time.

A PSYCHOLOGY OF FALLING AWAY FROM THE FAITH .... .65
Adrian van Kaam

A rare insight into this problem by a theologian with a psychologically oriented background.

UNDERSTANDING AND ACCEPTING OURSELVES AND OTHERS .65
William Zeller

Self-knowledge is important for mental health. Healthful growth of the individual depends on social development.

WHAT'S WRONG WITH GOD .65
Thomas M. Steeman

A probing search into a question that has practical ramifications for the modern man.

HELPING THE DISTURBED RELIGIOUS .65
E. F. Doherty

Like everybody else religious have problems of tensions and anxieties. Their causes and manner of handling are treated with sensitive insight.

WORLD POVERTY . . . CAN IT BE SOLVED? .65
Barbara Ward

In depth analysis of the problem of world poverty with sensible suggestions on how to solve it.

THE PRIESTHOOD: MASCULINE AND CELIBATE .65
Conrad W. Baars, M.D.

Psychiatrist, author, and consultant on the problems of the priesthood at the 1971 Vatican Synod of Bishops, Dr. Baars develops the positive values of celibacy and a regimen to achieve a priesthood both celibate and masculine.

THE RIDDLE OF GENESIS .65
Robert Koch

The study of comparative religion and modern biblical exegesis help to convey the essential message of the first eleven chapters of Genesis.

THE CHURCH TODAY .65

Important studies by men like Ratzinger, Schweizer, Congar, Pauwels and Winkhofer on various aspects of the Church in the modern world.

GROWTH TO MATURITY .65
Peter Cantwell O.F.M.

Maturity is not an accident of living. It is an achievement whose roots reach back to the very beginning of life, and are nurtured in successive stages.

THE DEFINITION OF THE CHRISTIAN LAYMAN .65
Edward Schillebeeckx O.P.

This author has established his right to speak with authority on a subject that is very important today. He bases his observations of Vatican II documents.

THE QUESTION OF FAITH IN THE RESURRECTION OF JESUS .65
Leonardo Boff O.F.M.

There have been many new interpretations of the Resurrection of Christ. These are investigated and contrasted with traditional belief.

HOW TO TREAT AND PREVENT THE CRISIS IN THE PRIESTHOOD .65
Conrad Baars, M.D.

A well-known psychiatrist, from vast experiences, discusses the role of the Church in the causation, treatment and prevention of the crisis in the priesthood.

FROM RESENTMENT TO GRATITUDE .65
Henri J. M. Nouwen

Challenges seminaries to overcome negative feelings and respond to life by a positive creative ministry.

THE MESSAGE OF CHRIST AND THE COUNSELOR $1.50
John Quesnel

An expert discusses the principles of counseling in general and pastoral counseling in particular as gleaned from the life of Christ.

TEMPTATIONS FOR THE
THEOLOGY OF LIBERATION .65
Bonaventure Kloppenburg O.F.M.

A member of the Papal Theological Commission warns against the various temptations to water-down, distort or belittle theology and the Gospel message. A clear voice in babel of confusion.

THE FAMILY PLANNING
DILEMMA REVISITED .65
John G. Quesnell

Since the publication of **Humane Vitae** a lot of study has been given to family planning. This booklet looks at the new insights in the light of the teaching of the Church. His is an optimistic approach.

RENEWAL AND RECONCILIATION .65
Reflections for a Holy Year
Msgr. James O'Reilly

The world, the Church, the family and society plus the sacramental system are discussed within the context of renewal and reconciliation. These reflections are appropriate for any year.

POLITICAL STRUGGLE OF ACTIVE
HOMOSEXUALS TO GAIN SOCIAL
ACCEPTANCE $1.50
George Kelly

Having learned from civil rights movements, overt homosexuals are exerting strong and expert political pressure to affect public mores.

CHARISMATIC RENEWAL IN
HISTORICAL PERSPECTIVE .65
John Carroll Futrell, S.J.

The Charismatic movement is recognized as good, authentic experience of the action of the Holy Spirit. The movement needs solid theology and orthodox biblical foundation. Risks are noted.

TO WHOM SHALL WE GO? .65
Zachary Hayes O.F.M.

Christ and the mystery of man is the theme of this booklet. It fills a gap as it focuses on the place of Christology in the Church today.

THE MORAL PROBLEMS OF CONTRACEPTION .65
Msgr. James O'Reilly

This booklet discusses the objective morality, without imputing subjective blame, of the contraceptive act. Contraception is regarded as a devaluation of a basic human good, namely the power to initiate human life.

COUNSELING TODAYS YOUTH $1.95
Peter Cantwell O.F.M.

With obvious expertise the author discusses the problems of modern youth and modern parents. He offers some practical suggestions in dealing with these problems.

THE SPIRITUAL DIRECTOR $1.50
Damien Isabell O.F.M.

This is a practical guide for spiritual direction on which growth depends. It contains an overview of approaches and an invaluable bibliography.

THE SACRAMENT OF PENANCE AND RECONCILIATION 65¢
Msgr. George A. Kelly

This is a sociological and historical study of the changes of attitude and practice of the Sacrament of Reconciliation.

THE HOMOSEXUAL'S SEARCH FOR HAPPINESS .65

Conrad W. Baars, M.D.

In this psycho-philosophical approach Dr. Baars treats homosexuality with remarkable compassion and understanding. He points out that the pressing need is personal, individual affirmation.

THE NATURE AND MEANING OF CHASTITY .65

William E. May, Ph.D.

Chastity is a loving integration of sex and affectivity into our lives enabling us, as sexual beings, to love and be loved. This definition is explained in detail.

LAY AND RELIGIOUS STATES OF LIFE: THEIR DISTINCTION AND COMPLEMENTARITY .65

James O'Reilly

The distinction between the lay and religious states of life must be maintained because of the nature of the movement of man toward salvation and the effect of the environment of life in the world.

THE PASCHAL MYSTERY: CORE GRACE IN THE LIFE OF THE CHRISTIAN .65

Augustine Paul Hennessy C.P.

Christian hope lies in the Risen Christ. Christians must learn to take on Christ's attitude toward the cross and the glory of it.

VALUING SUFFERING AS A CHRISTIAN: SOME PSYCHOLOGICAL PERSPECTIVES .65

Henry C. Simmons C.P.

Within the mystery of the cross of Christ, the sufferings of daily life hold meaning and value. Christian hope lies in the promises of Christ's death and resurrection.

SEX, LOVE AND PROCREATION .... .65
William E. May

This booklet is concerned with the important question: Can sexual intercourse as an act of love ever be separated from intercourse as a creative act?

AN UNCERTAIN CHURCH
THE NEW CATHOLIC PROBLEM .... .65
George A. Kelly and John A. Flynn

In a clear, concise manner this booklet explores the foundations of academic freedom. It is also a reaffirmation of the great Catholic heritage in intellectual circles.

MINIMUM ORDER $5.00